Piano/Vocal/Guitar •

GW01373059

# Walt Disney's

# Songs From The
# ARISTOCATS

## HAL•LEONARD®
### CORPORATION

7777 W. BLUEMOUND RD. P.O. BOX 13819 MILWAUKEE, WI 53213

# EV'RYBODY WANTS TO BE A CAT

Words by FLOYD HUDDLESTON
Music by AL RINKER

# EV'RYBODY WANTS TO BE A CAT

Words by FLOYD HUDDLESTON
Music by AL RINKER

6

# THE ARISTOCATS

Words and Music by RICHARD M. SHERMAN
and ROBERT B. SHERMAN

Which pet's ad - dress is the fin - est in Pa -
Which pets are blessed with the fair - est forms and

D.S. *Instrumental solo*

ris? Which pets pos - sess the long - est ped - i -
fac - es? Which pets know best all the gen - tle so - cial

gree? Which pets get to sleep on vel - vet
grac - es? Which pets live on cream and lov - ing

# SHE NEVER FELT ALONE

Words and Music by RICHARD M. SHERMAN
and ROBERT B. SHERMAN

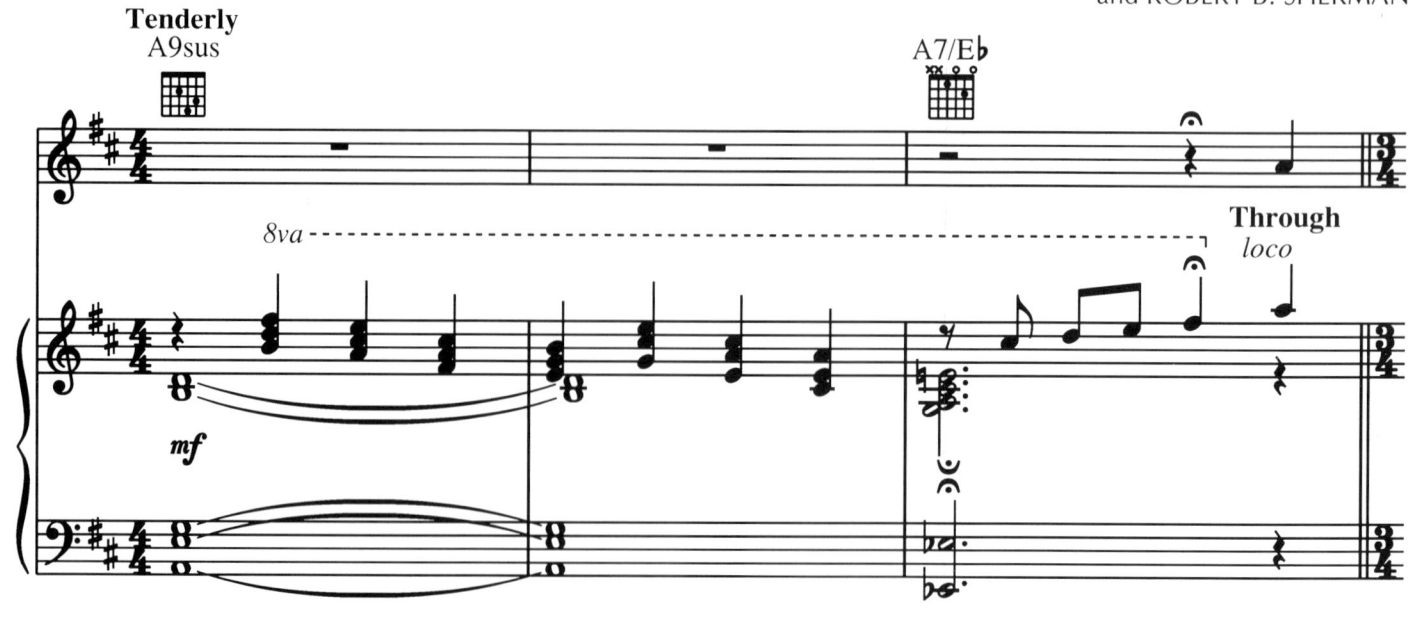

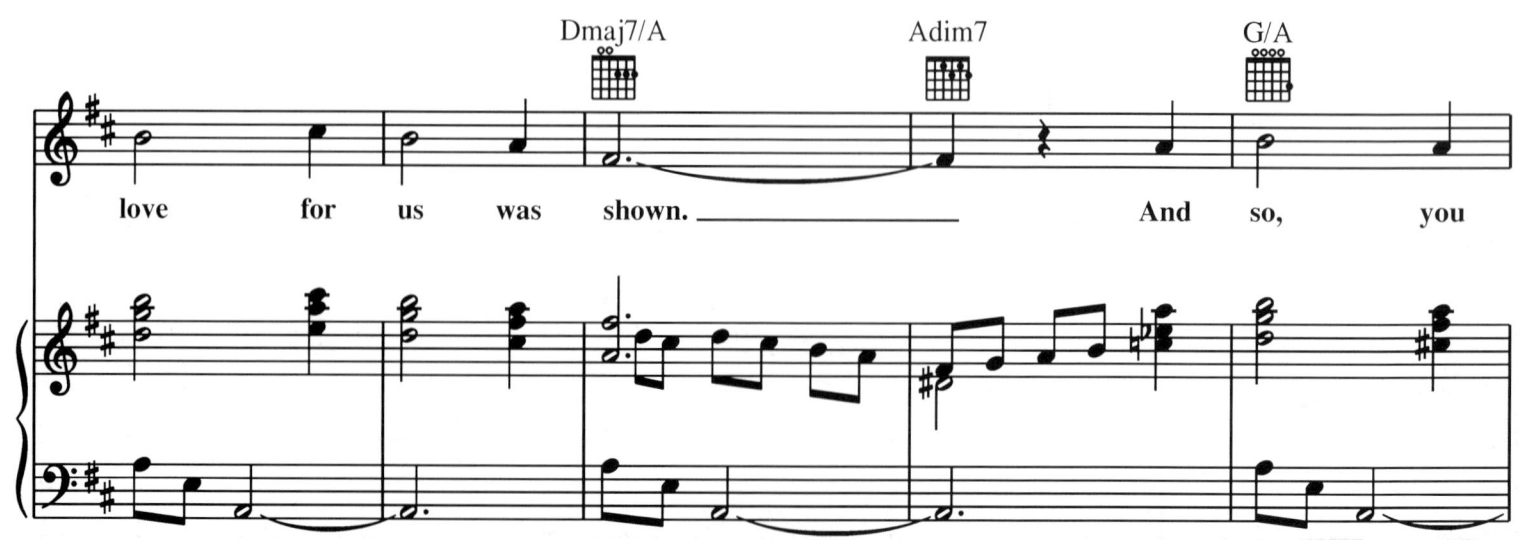

see, we can't leave her a - lone. _____

She'd al - ways say that we're the

great - est treas - ure she could own. _____ Be -

cause with us, she nev - er felt a - lone. _____

(Spoken:) *I'm so sorry, my dear, but we just have to go home.*

# THOMAS O'MALLEY CAT

Words and Music by
TERRY GILKYSON

# SCALES AND ARPEGGIOS

Words and Music by RICHARD M. SHERMAN
and ROBERT B. SHERMAN

F    F#dim7

To Coda

Bring the mu - sic ring - ing from your chest and not your nose
Do mi so mi do mi so mi fa la so it goes
If you're smart, you'll learn by heart what

1
C/G    G7    C

while you sing your scales and your ar - peg - gi - os.

2
C/G    G7    C

when you do the scales and your ar - peg - gi - os.

G7    C